NICOLE POWERS, MSN, PMHNP-BC

HE SEES ME, TOO

30 DAYS OF DEVOTIONS, PRAYERS, AND REFLECTIONS FOR PARENTS AND CAREGIVERS CALLED TO SHEPHERD SPECIAL NEEDS CHILDREN

NICOLE POWERS, MSN, PMHNP-BC

HE SEES ME, TOO

30 DAYS OF DEVOTIONS, PRAYERS, AND REFLECTIONS FOR PARENTS AND CAREGIVERS CALLED TO SHEPHERD SPECIAL NEEDS CHILDREN

He Sees Me Too by Nicole Powers.

ISBN: 979-8-950053-02-3

Published in the United States by Yosi Publishing, LLC. For more inquiries or permissions, please contact the publisher at www.yosipublishing.com

Cover Design by Kai Holmes-Cooks of Kai&Co.

To God, thank You for guiding us through every trial and blessing us with the courage to embrace our uniqueness. Your grace nourishes our souls and lights our path, reminding us that we are never alone on this journey. I love You deeply and thank You for entrusting me with Your children.

To my beloved children, your laughter and resilience inspire me every single day. You have taught me the true meaning of love, joy, and perseverance. This devotional stands as a testament to your strength and spirit, a reminder that together we can face any challenge. To my twins, Kayden and Kellen—you have taught me more than I could ever teach you. I wouldn't change a thing about our journey. We love you beyond words.

To all the special needs parents, this book is for you—the warriors who navigate the complexities of raising extraordinary children. Your unwavering love, your trials, and your triumphs inspire me. My prayer is that the stories in these pages bring you solace, encouragement, and hope. Remember, we walk this path together, united in both our challenges and our victories.

With love and gratitude,
Nicole

Contents

Introduction

The morning sun slips through my curtains, painting the walls of our small, cozy living room in soft gold. The air carries the warm scent of coffee, mingling with the sweet aroma of cinnamon oatmeal bubbling on the stove. My praise and worship playlist hums in the background as the kettle begins its familiar whistle. From the playroom, I hear the music of my twins' laughter—Kayden and Kellen—though they are not playing with each other, but beside each other. That small detail has always lingered in my mind.

Beneath their radiant smiles and pure giggles lived a reality I would come to know well: they inhabited their own worlds, even while standing in mine.

I remember the day their worlds gained a name. Dr. Frazier sat across from me, her voice calm but steady, as she said, "They have autism spectrum disorder." The words floated in the air like heavy clouds. My heart stalled, holding back tears that threatened to spill. I had worked with teens and adults diagnosed with autism in my career as a Psychiatric Mental Health Nurse Practitioner, but nothing prepared me to hear those words about my own children.

The exam room fell silent except for the ticking clock, its steady rhythm mocking my scrambled thoughts. Outside, the scent of blooming jasmine mixed with birdsong—a beauty that felt almost cruel against the storm inside me. I strapped my boys into their car seats, watching them fiddle with toys, blissfully unaware of how life had just shifted. Their laughter filled the truck, a melody both comforting and bittersweet. I knew then this journey—whatever it would hold—was ours to walk, and God would walk it with us.

Our Everyday World

Life became a mosaic of triumphs and trials.

Bright reds and greens of toy blocks scattered across the carpet. Blue storybook covers worn soft from endless readings. The calming feel of their soft curls between my fingers after a long day.

In one moment, we faced meltdowns like sudden thunderstorms; in another, we found quiet peace in bedtime lullabies or evening cups of tea. Our home became both sanctuary and classroom, a place where love and patience were tested and deepened.

Some evenings, we drew chalk masterpieces on the driveway, giggling under the shade of rustling leaves. Other days, I felt the weight of societal expectations pressing in—navigating therapies, Individualized Education Program (IEP) meetings, and the unspoken questions of strangers. Yet through every obstacle, I found a strength I didn't know I had, rooted in the presence of God and my love for my sons.

Becoming Their Advocate

Their challenges did not define them; their beauty did. I became their fiercest advocate, standing guard against misconceptions and judgments. Every milestone—a new word, a shared smile, a peaceful outing—was cause for celebration. These moments, small to others, were monumental for us.

Motherhood, especially in this space, taught me that love knows no limits. Kayden and Kellen's innocence, curiosity, and unfiltered joy changed me. They gave me the courage to connect deeply with other parents on this path, and to extend a hand of hope.

Why This Devotional Exists

In the quiet moments of exhaustion—when the air felt thick with anxiety and I wondered if anyone truly saw me—God whispered, "I see you." That truth became the heartbeat of this devotional, *He Sees Me Too*.

This is more than a book. It is a safe space for special needs parents and caretakers to find encouragement and connection. It is an honest account of life's trials and triumphs, written from the heart of a single mother who has walked this road and found God's grace at every bend. And it is a daily reminder that you are not invisible—not to me, and not to God.

What to Expect Each Day

Over the next 30 days, we will walk together—through vulnerability, hope, and faith. Each day is designed to meet you exactly where you are, with four sacred spaces to anchor your heart:

He Knows Me, Too: where God's Word speaks directly into your story, knowing you fully before you even find the words.

He Feels Me, Too: a devotional reflection from my heart to yours, where we sit honestly in the weight and wonder of this journey together.

He Sees Me, Too: a moment to pause, reflect, and journal, anchoring your spirit in the truth that God's eyes never leave you or your children.

He Hears Me, Too: a prayer to close each day, lifting your voice to a God who leans in close and listens.

You are not alone in this journey. We rise together. We grow together. And we embrace the truth—He *knows* you, He *feels* you, He *sees* you, and He *hears* you, too.

1

Not Just Their Healer—Mine Too

He Knows Me, Too

And the people, when they knew it, followed Him: and He received them, and spake unto them of the kingdom of God, and healed them that had need of healing *(Luke 9:11, KJV).*

He Feels Me, Too

There are moments in life that ache in places too deep for words—moments when the heart is heavy, the mind overwhelmed, and the soul quietly pleading for rest. As a mother of twin boys on the autism spectrum, I know those moments well.

Some days, the healing I needed wasn't just physical. It was emotional. It was spiritual. It was mental. There were nights I whispered prayers through tears, days I fought back fear in silence, and countless moments when worship was the only thing holding me together.

I'll never forget the day one of my sons slipped out of the house. One moment, the stillness felt harmless. The next, it screamed danger. The front door was cracked, and my heart plummeted.

I sprinted barefoot down the hot sidewalk, calling his name until my voice broke. I banged on doors, begging for help, while neighbors peered out in confusion and concern. All I could think was, *"Please, Lord—not the street, not the pond, not the woods."*

And then—I saw him. Fifteen houses down. Standing in the grass, staring up at the sky, smiling as if he had discovered a secret place only he and God knew.

I ran. I scooped him into my arms and held him so tightly I could barely breathe. And on that sidewalk, I wept. Not just because of fear, but because of the crushing weight of this journey. The tears carried more than panic. They carried my questions. *"God, will he ever speak? Will I always live in fear? Am I enough for this? God, can you heal me, too?"* That day, I realized something: I wasn't just praying for my son's healing. I was crying out for mine.

Parenting a child with special needs isn't just about appointments, therapies, and advocacy. It's about surrendering daily. It's about trusting that the same Jesus who heals our children is reaching for us, too.

Maybe you have had a moment like this—a moment where your fear for your child cracked open a deeper cry for yourself. You are not alone in that.

Our tears are a language all their own and God understands every drop. He interprets what we cannot speak, feels what we cannot express, and meets us in the places words cannot reach. And that cry—the one you whispered through tears, the one you swallowed in silence—God felt every word of it. He has not missed a single moment of your pain, and He is not finished healing you yet.

He Sees Me, Too

Parenting a child with special needs is sacred work. It's holy ground walked in bare feet, soaked in tears, and covered in grace. It will stretch you, break you, and reveal just how much you need God to carry the pieces you can't hold. He is not just your child's Healer—He sees your need, and He is reaching for you, too.

Take a moment to reflect honestly:

- Where do I need healing as a parent today?
- Have I silently wondered if I'm enough—for this child, for this calling?
- In what areas am I asking God to heal me, not just

my children?

Write your answers freely. This is not about polished prayers or perfect words. It's about releasing what's heavy and allowing the Healer to fill the missing pieces of your soul.

You are not failing. You are not alone. God sees every meltdown, every therapy session, every sleepless night, and every whispered prayer. He chose you for this journey, and He is not just your child's Healer—He is yours too.

____

____

____

____

____

____

____

____

____

____

____

____

____

____

____

____

____

____

____

____

____

____

____

____

He Hears Me, Too

Father, we come before You with open hearts and trembling hands. We ask for Your mercy, grace, and supernatural healing. Touch our children, Lord, in every place that needs Your divine hand. But also, heal us—the parents. Restore our strength when we feel weak. Wrap our minds in peace when fear tries to consume us. Let Your light steady us in the darkest moments. May our lives shine as a testimony of Your power and love. And may You always receive the glory. In Jesus' Name, Amen.

2

Strength When I'm Empty

He Knows Me, Too

He giveth power to the faint; and to them that have no might He increaseth strength *(Isaiah 40:29, KJV).*

He Feels Me, Too

There are days when being a single mother to my twin boys feels like more than I can carry. I remember sitting in the quiet of the night, the house finally still, my eyes burning with exhaustion and my body aching from the day. I would ask myself questions I didn't dare say out loud: *Will my sons ever speak? Will their behaviors ever calm? Will they always need someone to care for them when I'm gone?*

Those "what ifs" pressed on me like heavy bricks, keeping me awake long after midnight. My mind raced, circling through futures I couldn't control, while my heart begged God for answers. I felt drained, my spirit faint.

The truth is, some days I still feel depleted—mentally tapped out, barely able to stand another tantrum or meltdown. I've been through it all: an hour of screaming until their little throats were raw, their bodies banging against walls, their tiny hands leaving scratches on my arms, or watching them tear the house apart—cabinet doors hanging, shelves yanked from the fridge, the weight of chaos heavy in the air.

There was one winter where I survived on two hours of sleep for weeks at a time. My reflection in the mirror showed bags under my eyes that seemed older than I was. And I whispered, "God, I can't keep going. This is too much for me."

And every time, He met me there. Not always with instant answers, but with strength I didn't have the moment before. His voice reminded me, "I'm right here. Get back up—I'm walking with you through this."

It's not easy. Parenting children with special needs rarely is. But Isaiah 40:29 is a promise I hold tight: when my might runs out, His power steps in.

He Sees Me, Too

Take a moment today to be honest with God and yourself. You don't need perfect words—just an open heart.

- Where do you feel most depleted right now?
- What "what ifs" have been weighing on your heart and stealing your rest?
- In what ways do you need God's strength to step in today?

Write your reflections below. Let this be your release—a place where you don't have to hold it all together. Remember, His strength increases where yours ends.

____

____

____

____

____

____

____

____

____

____

____

____

____

____

____

____

____

____

____

____

____

____

____

____

He Hears Me, Too

Father, thank You for being my strength when I have none left. You see every tear, every sleepless night, every meltdown, and every weary sigh. Today I surrender my "what ifs" and my fears into Your hands. Wrap me in Your peace, and remind me that You are walking with me through every trial. Strengthen my body, calm my mind, and steady my spirit so I can love my children the way You've called me to. In Jesus' Name, Amen.

3

Waiting on My Miracle

He Knows Me, Too

And said, If thou wilt diligently hearken to the voice of the Lord thy God, and wilt do that which is right in His sight, and wilt give ear to His commandments, and keep all His statutes, I will put none of these diseases upon thee, which I have brought upon the Egyptians: for I am the Lord that healeth thee *(Exodus 15:26, KJV).*

He Feels Me, Too

I hold tightly to the promise that God is the Lord who heals. I remind myself of it on the days when my body feels heavy with exhaustion, and my heart aches with waiting.

When my boys were babies, something in me knew early on that something was different. At ten months old, when other children were babbling "mama" or "dada," mine sat in silence. My spirit stirred, and the Holy Spirit whispered, *"Get on it right away."* I didn't hesitate. I enrolled them in early intervention. By the time they were two and a half, both were diagnosed with autism. The waitlist for therapy was long, and the nights were longer.

I remember those days vividly. The air thick with the sharp scent of bleach after cleaning the walls. The sound of tiny feet climbing onto tables, the thud of small bodies against corners, and the mess that broke me down to tears—poop smeared on walls, in places I never imagined. Irregular cries filled the house, sounds I couldn't always understand. Food became a battle—textures turned into tears, chicken nuggets and fries the only safe ground. I learned quickly that when their little bodies were constipated, their behaviors flared—screeches, head-banging, and fits that left us all trembling.

But God. Today, I see His hand. One of my sons—Kayden—graduated from his autism school in Spring

2025. He speaks fluently now, full sentences flowing like music I once thought I'd never hear. The boy who couldn't say "Mom" now calls for me with joy in his voice. No more therapies. No more delays. In September, he will walk into a regular elementary school. He is kind, mild-mannered, full of hugs and kisses, and truly the life of the party.

God healed him. He showed me He had not forgotten me.

Now, I wait for the same miracle for his brother. He's making eye contact, saying single words, and I believe with everything in me that his victory is on the way.

God is a miracle worker. I've seen Him do it before, and I know He will do it again.

He Sees Me, Too

Healing doesn't always happen all at once. Sometimes it comes piece by piece, like a puzzle slowly forming the picture God already sees completed.

Take time today to reflect and write:

- Where have you seen glimpses of God's healing in your life or in your child's life?
- What promises are you still holding onto, even if you haven't seen the full picture yet?
- How can you remind yourself today that God has *not forgotten you*?

Write honestly, even if your healing still feels "in progress." Your words are safe here.

He Hears Me, Too

Father, thank You for being a merciful and faithful God. Thank You for every glimpse of healing, every step forward, and every promise You are fulfilling in Your perfect timing. I surrender the weight of waiting into Your hands. Strengthen my faith as I trust You for the miracles still to come. Remind me that Your plan for my children is already secured in Heaven. I declare that Your perfect will shall be done. In Jesus' Name, Amen.

4

When Tears Speak Louder Than Words

He Knows Me, Too

And ye shall serve the Lord your God, and He shall bless thy bread, and thy water; and I will take sickness away from the midst of thee *(Exodus 23:25, KJV)*.

He Feels Me, Too

Some moments in life are etched into your memory forever. For me, one of those moments came on a hot Friday afternoon at Short Pump Mall. The sun was blazing, the summer crowd thick, laughter and chatter bouncing through the air. People strolled in and out of stores with shopping bags swinging, their faces carefree. But for one mother—and for me—that day was anything but ordinary.

I noticed her first because I knew the look. Her cheeks were flushed, her breath short and uneven, her eyes wide with desperation. She was in her 40s or 50s, pleasantly plump, with salt-and-pepper hair pulled back, her skin damp with sweat. Her little boy—about the same size as my twins—was on the ground, banging his head against the hard concrete. His red cheeks streaked with tears, his mushroom haircut falling into his eyes, his blue t-shirt and sandals damp with the heat of the day.

People stared. Some snickered. Others raised their phones to film, their whispers and sideways glances louder than any words. Not one offered to help. I could see the mortified look on her face as she whispered, *"Billy, stop…"* her voice breaking, her body heaving with exhaustion.

I didn't think twice. I walked over, and without a word, I wrapped my arms around her. For ten minutes, in the middle of that crowded mall, we held onto each other and cried. The kind of tears that don't need explaining. The kind that come from a place too deep for words. Her son looked up at us, and for a moment, he stopped. No more banging. Just quiet.

It was as if our tears had spoken louder than the stares, louder than the judgment, louder than the chaos. In that hug, there was a silent understanding: *I see you. I know. You are not alone.*

Being a parent to children with special needs means even simple outings can feel like battles. It's a daily test of faith, of strength, of endurance. Yet even in the hardest moments, I remind myself of what God has promised me: both of my sons will be healed and restored. His Word says He will take sickness away. And His Word never lies.

So I hold onto that truth—even when the world is watching, even when the tears fall in public places, even when I don't have the strength to say a word.

He Sees Me, Too

Think back on a time when you felt seen in the middle of your struggle—or when you saw someone else and offered them strength without words.

- Who in your life has God sent as a reminder that you are not alone?

- How can you be that reminder for another parent walking this journey?

- What promises from God are you holding onto, even when the evidence hasn't yet matched the vision?

Write your reflections here. Let the page carry your heart so you don't have to carry it all alone.

He Hears Me, Too

Father, we come before You with humble hearts, grateful that You see us in the crowd when no one else does. Thank You for every promise in Your Word and for the reminders that we are not alone in this journey. Heal our hearts from doubt and guilt. Strengthen us for the days that feel too heavy. Use us to be a light for other parents, just as others have been a light for us. We surrender every moment—every meltdown, every tear, every hug—into Your hands. In Jesus' Name, Amen.

5

Why Not Us?

He Knows Me, Too

And the Lord will take away from thee all sickness, and will put none of the evil diseases of Egypt, which thou knowest upon thee; but will lay them upon all them that hate thee *(Deuteronomy 7:15, KJV).*

He Feels Me, Too

It was a Friday evening at Wegmans, around six o'clock. The aisles were crowded, the air heavy with the smell of fresh bread and rotisserie chicken. I was picking up ingredients for a seafood boil, pushing my twins through the store.

The lights seemed brighter than usual, the chatter of other shoppers louder, and I felt the day pressing down on me.

Then it happened. One of my boys suddenly shifted in the cart. His body twisted as if overtaken by an unseen force. He pulled at his shirt, his face red, his little body jerking with intensity. In seconds, the meltdown spiraled. Oranges flew from his tiny hands, bouncing off shelves and rolling across the floor. Some hit other shoppers, who gasped and recoiled. His teeth sank into my shoulder, and my whole body stung with pain. Then he banged his head against the cart, the sound echoing like a drumbeat of desperation.

The entire store froze. People stared. Whispers filled the air like a low hum. The store manager approached, irritation written all over his face. "I'm sorry, ma'am, but we're going to have to ask you to leave. You're upsetting our customers." His tone cut me deeper than the stares.

One elderly woman shook her head and muttered, *"My God, will someone get him?"* Her words weren't filled with compassion, but judgment—because she didn't know. She didn't know my child was autistic. She didn't know the daily battles we faced. She didn't know the weight I carried.

I held it together until we made it to the truck. Then I crumbled. Tears poured down my face as I cried out, "God, what did I do to deserve this? Why is my child like this? I hate all of it! I wish I was dead! No one understands. No one cares."

And then I heard it. A voice—gentle, firm, unmistakable. "Are you done? This is not about you or your sons. I am doing something in and through you. You will help others with this very thing. But first, you must walk through it."

In that moment, the weight shifted. I realized this journey wasn't punishment. It was purpose. From that day on, I stopped asking, "Why me?" and started asking, "Why not us?"

We are generational curse breakers. And though the nights are long and the meltdowns still come, I trust that God is working all things for our good.

He Sees Me, Too

It's easy to let bitterness take root when the weight of parenting a child with special needs feels unbearable. But surrender opens the door for healing.

Take time today to reflect:

- Have I ever felt bitterness or resentment toward God because of my child's diagnosis?
- What would it look like for me to live from a place of surrender instead of frustration?
- Where can I see evidence—even small glimpses—that God is doing something in and through my journey?

Write honestly. This is not about shame—it's about release.

He Hears Me, Too

Father, You are the One who perfects all things in Your time. Even when this is not what we prayed for or expected, we thank You for the gift of parenting these precious children. Like Hannah dedicated Samuel, today we dedicate our children to You, believing they will be living testimonies of Your goodness in the earth. Heal our hearts from bitterness. Replace our "why me" with "why not us." Strengthen us as we walk in the calling You have placed on our lives. In Jesus' Name, Amen.

6

Whose Report Will You Believe?

He Knows Me, Too

And it shall come to pass, if thou shalt hearken diligently unto the voice of the Lord thy God, to observe and to do all His commandments which I command thee this day, that the Lord thy God will set thee on high above all nations of the earth: And all these blessings shall come on thee, and overtake thee, if thou shalt hearken unto the voice of the Lord thy God *(Deuteronomy 28:1-2, KJV).*

He Feels Me, Too

I'll never forget the day a neurologist in his seventies looked me in the eye and told me my twins would never talk. He said one might not even walk. His words were flat, clinical, delivered like a verdict. He spoke about milestones they hadn't met, about group homes when they grew older, about limitations that sounded like a life sentence.

I sat there with my babies in my arms, their warm little bodies pressed against me, and I knew I had a choice: to accept man's report or to believe God's.

With every word he spoke, I whispered inside myself, "No. That is not their story. That is not our future." I refused to take his report as truth. Instead, I spoke life: "They will talk. They will walk. They will thrive. God has the final say."

The road wasn't easy. There were long nights of prayer, early intervention appointments, and days when the weight of waiting felt unbearable. But I clung to the Word of God like oxygen. And I saw Him move.

Today, both of my sons are walking, running, full of life. One speaks fluently—sentences rolling off his tongue like a song I once thought I'd never hear. The other is making strides every day, forming words, growing stronger. Healing is happening right before my eyes.

If I had accepted the doctor's report, I don't know where we'd be. But because I believed the Lord's, I can testify today: His Word never fails.

So, I ask you—whose report will you believe?

He Sees Me, To

Take a few quiet minutes to reflect and write:

- What words have been spoken over you or your child that you need to reject today?
- What promises from God are you choosing to believe instead?
- Beyond parenting, what has God called you to do that requires full submission and trust in Him?

Write from the lens of faith, not fear. Let your words declare the truth of who you are and what God has spoken over your family.

____

____

____

____

____

____

____

He Hears Me, Too

Father, You are faithful and true. Thank You for reminding us that You—and You alone—have the final say over our lives and our children's lives. Teach us to walk boldly in our calling and to trust Your report above every other voice. Give us courage to reject fear and embrace faith, and let our lives be living testimonies of Your healing power. We give You all the glory. In Jesus' Name, Amen.

7

Promises Worth Waiting For

He Knows Me, Too

For I know the thoughts that I think toward you, saith the Lord, thoughts of peace, and not of evil, to give you an expected end *(Jeremiah 29:11, KJV).*

He Feels Me, Too

When I think about my children's future, I remind myself of this truth: God's plan is better than mine. Even when the weight of parenting six children alone feels like more than I can bear—even when two of those children are twins on the autism spectrum—I know His thoughts toward us are of peace and not of evil. He holds the blueprint of their lives in His hands.

I'll be honest. There were moments when I asked God, "Is this payback? Did I do something wrong to deserve this?" My tears would fall heavy, and I felt the urge to give up—like leaving it all behind. But in those moments, His voice would steady me: *"This is not punishment. You are going to help many people. You cannot give up. You will live the life of purpose I've called you to."*

A friend once told me, "You have so much grace with your children." I didn't always see it, but I've learned that grace doesn't always feel soft—it often feels like grit, like getting back up after sleepless nights, tantrums, and long therapy appointments.

I've been a mother since I was 20, and now in my 40s, I know that no child can be parented the same way. My girls need one-on-one time, personal date days, deep talks where I can hear their hearts. My boys need patience, structure, and unconditional love. Every child is different, yet God reminds me: *"None will be left behind. I see them all. I see you."*

He also reminds me, "Just because you're single doesn't mean you're alone. The Holy Spirit is your guide, and I am with you."

I have not missed a beat yet—not because it's been easy, but because God's promises never fail. So I keep holding on. I remind myself daily: it may not happen on my timeline, but it will happen. Healing will come. Purpose will unfold. And God will get the glory.

He Sees Me, Too

God's promises are certain, even when the waiting feels endless. Take a moment to reflect and write:

- What has God spoken to you about your children's future?

- How do you remind yourself of His promises when discouragement sets in?

- What dreams, visions, or goals has He placed in your heart that you've put aside—and how might He be calling you to pick them back up?

Write freely, with faith, even if you haven't yet seen the promise fulfilled.

____

____

____

____

____

____

____

____

____

____

____

____

____

____

____

____

____

____

____

____

____

____

____

He Hears Me, Too

Father, thank You that You are not a man that You should lie, nor the son of man that You should repent. Every word You speak is sure. Today we choose to trust Your timing and Your promises, even when the wait feels long. Teach us to parent with faith, strength, and grace, knowing You are guiding our steps. We surrender our dreams, our children, and our future into Your hands. We wait with expectation for the fulfillment of every promise You've spoken. In Jesus' Name, Amen.

8

Finding Joy in the Middle of It All

He Knows Me, Too

Delight thyself also in the Lord; and He shall give thee the desires of thine heart *(Psalm 37:4, KJV)*.

He Feels Me, Too

There was a time when I thought the safest thing to do was stay home. Sundays when there wasn't a children's church for my twins, I'd livestream the service instead of risking a meltdown in the sanctuary. Grocery trips had to be timed like a mission—never too crowded, never too late, or else chaos could break out in the aisles. The list of places I avoided grew longer, and before I realized it, isolation had become my way of life.

But one day, God whispered to me: "I made everyone differently, but I never made you to hide. Lean into community. There are parents out there who need you—and who you need too."

It wasn't easy, but I listened. I started stepping out in faith, asking God to cover my children and calm my heart before every outing. I prayed over my boys daily—not just for their healing, but for peace, protection, and strength for all of us.

I'll never forget the birthday party my six-year-old was invited to. I walked in with my guard up, nerves buzzing through me like electricity. I scanned the room, already bracing for stares or whispers if one of my twins had a meltdown. But what I found was unexpected: six other mothers, each raising a child on the spectrum. We started talking, sharing our stories, and by the end of the party, we had exchanged numbers.

I left that day lighter than I'd arrived. I wasn't the only one. God reminded me, "When you delight in Me, I'll give you not just what you need, but even the desires of your heart—even if that desire is simply not to feel alone."

Now, when I step into spaces that once made me anxious, I do so with prayer on my lips and faith in my heart. Because I know this truth: our home may be our first ministry, but God also calls us to live boldly beyond our walls. And in Him, isolation has no place.

He Sees Me, Too

Think about the desires in your heart right now.

- Are they rooted in God's will, or in your own plans?

- Where have you isolated yourself out of fear or exhaustion, and how might God be calling you back into community?

- How can you "delight in the Lord" today—in a way that shifts your focus from the struggle to His promises?

Write honestly. Don't filter. God delights in your truth and meets you right where you are.

____

____

____

____

____

____

____

____

____

____

____

____

____

____

____

____

____

____

____

____

____

____

____

He Hears Me, Too

Father, thank You for holding our future in Your hands. Teach us to make You the center of our lives and to delight in You in every season. When fear tempts us to isolate, remind us that You designed us for community. Cover our children, our homes, and our hearts with Your peace. Thank You for being the God of miracles, the One who turns isolation into connection, and sorrow into joy. We love You, we trust You, and we worship You. In Jesus' Name, Amen.

9

The Morning Peace Spoke Loudest

He Knows Me, Too

And the peace of God, which passeth all understanding, shall keep your hearts and minds through Christ Jesus *(Philippians 4:7, KJV).*

He Feels Me, Too

There's a peace that can't be explained — a peace that settles into your bones even when life looks nothing like you thought it would. I've learned to find that peace when I'm deep in God's Word, petitioning on behalf of my twins. I pray with authority, knowing that if I ask according to His will, it is already done.

It has always been God's will that our children walk in freedom and victory. But I had to come to a place of surrender — handing their futures and their healing into His hands. I remember praying, *"Lord, I surrender. My desire is for my boys to talk, to live successful lives spiritually, mentally, and physically. But I trust Your timing. I believe all will be well."*

Four months later, God gave me a miracle.

It was a Saturday morning in early April 2024, just before their third birthday. The house was quiet, everyone still asleep. The spring air drifted through the window, cool and soft, while I sat in my home office finishing a Zoom session with a patient. Then I heard it.

A small voice behind me said, *"Mommy, I want to eat."*

I froze. The words rang in my ears like a melody I'd longed for but never heard. My heart stopped and then pounded so hard I thought it would break through my chest. Tears rushed to my eyes. I hung up on the patient mid-sentence and turned to see my son standing there, his eyes bright, his little face waiting for me to respond.

"Say it again," I whispered.

He did. And then I cried so loudly I woke up the whole house. My other children came running, their faces still sleepy, and when I told them, the tears spread. We all cried together — a flood of relief, of joy, of God's goodness breaking through our waiting.

My son, who had been completely nonverbal, spoke in full sentences. Just like that. Overnight.

That day, peace wrapped around me like a blanket. God had kept His promise. And while I'm still waiting for his twin brother to have his moment, I no longer carry the weight of fear. I know in God's timing, his day will come. Because once you've seen God move, you never forget the sound of His faithfulness.

He Sees Me, Too

Peace often shows up in the waiting, not in the answers.

Take time today to reflect and write:

- Where in your life has God surprised you with peace that didn't make sense?

- What miracles are you still waiting for — and how can peace guard your heart as you wait?

- How can you daily surrender your children's futures into God's hands?

Write honestly, letting God meet you in the quiet.

____

____

____

____

He Hears Me, Too

Lord, thank You for being the source of peace that surpasses all understanding. When anxious thoughts rise, remind me that You are faithful and present. Guard my mind from torment and help me think only on what is good and true.

I surrender my children's futures into Your hands and trust that in Your perfect time, every promise will be fulfilled. In Jesus' Name, Amen.

10

Wonderfully Made with Purpose

He Knows Me, Too

I will praise thee; for I am fearfully and wonderfully made: marvelous are thy works; and that my soul knoweth right well *(Psalm 139:14, KJV).*

He Feels Me, Too

Every one of my children is special in their own way, but my twins are something truly extraordinary. Watching the way they think, process, and interact with the world is like watching a glimpse of God's creativity at work. They amaze me—baby geniuses when it comes to anything electronic or tech. From the very beginning, I knew they carried a divine calling.

When my boys were nonverbal, they used Augmentative and Alternative Communication (AAC) devices—special speech tablets designed for children with autism or other speech challenges. Insurance covered them, and within three weeks of working with their speech therapist, I watched their faces light up as they pressed buttons and found their voices through those screens. "Wants chicken nuggets now..." the device would say, and I'd smile, knowing it was just a stepping stone.

Kaylyn carried his everywhere, while Kayden mainly used his at school. But both of them caught on so quickly, it was as if their minds had been waiting for this bridge to expression. Their therapist downloaded a program full of pictures and words, and every day they learned more. To the world, it might have looked like just a tablet. But to me, it was a promise in progress.

All the while, I spoke life over them. Every morning, every evening, every chance I got, I declared Job 22:28 over their lives: *"You are smart. You are strong. You are mighty men of God."* I decreed and declared their future even when their present seemed silent.

Because I knew this: they weren't just placed on this earth by chance. They were sent here with purpose—purpose to change me, to work through me, and to bless others. Each intricate part of their brains, each fiber of their being, was woven with the love and intention of God.

And I stand in awe that He chose me to mother them.

He Sees Me, Too

Look at your child today with fresh eyes.

- What is the first thing that comes to mind when you see them?
- Have you paused to give God glory for trusting you with them?
- Instead of focusing on the struggles, how can you celebrate the ways they are fearfully and wonderfully made?

Write your reflections. Let this be a place where you honor the divine design in your child—and remind yourself that God entrusted them to you for a reason.

____

____

____

____

____

____

____

He Hears Me, Too

Lord, thank You for creating my child fearfully and wonderfully, with intention and purpose. Help me to see them as You do—full of potential, gifts, and divine calling. Give me the wisdom and strength to nurture their purpose and develop their gifts as vessels to be used by You. I praise You for entrusting me with this honor. In Jesus' Name, Amen.

11

Strength in the Stillness

He Knows Me, Too

Come unto me, all ye that labour and are heavy laden, and I will give you rest *(Matthew 11:28, KJV).*

He Feels Me, Too

The day I received the autism diagnosis for my twins, my heart felt like it had shattered into pieces too heavy to gather. I remember lying in bed, the room dim even with the sun pouring through the blinds, tears soaking into my pillow. My mind was a battlefield. Thoughts raced like wild horses—accusations, doubts, fears, and guilt. *"This is your fault. You're not enough. You'll never get through this."* Satan was loud, and I felt powerless to silence him.

I couldn't see past that day, let alone imagine a week, a year, or a future. Darkness pressed in heavy. But even in that place, a whisper stirred: *"Get up. Call on Me."*

It took everything in me, but I did. I started praying, even when my voice trembled. I fasted, even when my flesh screamed. And slowly, God met me there.

It wasn't dramatic at first—no thunder, no lightning. Just stillness. And in that stillness, He gave me strategy. After prayer, I'd feel nudged to call a therapist, research a nutrition plan, schedule an appointment with a dentist or a barber who would understand my boys' needs. Sometimes it was as simple as knowing which door to knock on next.

I realized then: nothing would change if I stayed in that bed. My children needed more than my tears—they needed my fight. And I couldn't fight without God's strength.

The key was staying close—fervent prayer, consistent fasting, and quiet moments of listening. Some of my greatest breakthroughs came not from doing more, but from sitting in His presence, surrendering the weight I couldn't carry.

Now, when weariness creeps in, I run to Him first. My heart no longer feels heavy, because I know their healing is already on the way. Any day now, I believe, we'll see the full manifestation. Until then, I rest in the One who carries us all.

He Sees Me, Too

Take a moment today to pause and reflect:

- What burdens are you carrying that you need to lay at the feet of Jesus?
- When was the last time you allowed yourself to sit in God's stillness instead of pushing through in your own strength?
- What breakthroughs are you believing God for as you commit to prayer and fasting?

Write openly, without rushing. Let the stillness be a place where God gives you strength.

____

____

____

____

____

____

____

____

____

____

____

____

____

____

____

____

____

____

____

____

____

____

____

He Hears Me, Too

Lord, I bring my weariness to You. Refresh me with Your rest and fill me with the strength only You can give. When my mind grows heavy and my body feels weak, remind me that I don't have to carry this alone. Teach me to live through the lens of Christ, trusting Your plan even when I don't see it yet. Thank You for strategy, peace, and breakthrough. In Jesus' Name, Amen.

12

Building a Godly Foundation

He Knows Me, Too

Train up a child in the way he should go: and when he is old, he will not depart from it *(Proverbs 22:6, KJV).*

He Feels Me, Too

With six children and now a grandchild, I know how important it is that my household knows the Lord. God's Word is the roadmap to life, and setting a solid foundation has always been one of my greatest priorities as a mother.

Even with my twins' special needs, I've watched them learn to love God in ways that move me to tears. The Lord knows them deeply, and I see Him shaping their hearts.

Some of my favorite moments happen around our kitchen table. We'll go around, each child sharing one way they've seen God at work in their lives that week. Their voices fill the room—some soft, some loud, some hesitant—but each one precious. Then we dive into family Bible study, opening the Scriptures and reflecting on what the verses mean to them.

Just last month, I introduced "Bible Bingo." I spread flashcards across the table—each one with a verse reference. They draw a card, read the passage aloud, and place a coin on the verse if they find it in the Bible. The energy in the room is electric. They cheer, laugh, and lean forward eagerly, competing for the prize of a special mommy date. I always make sure everyone feels like a winner, but the joy of hearing them repeat God's Word—that's the true prize.

Week by week, I see it sinking in. They're forming habits of Scripture memory, learning not just verses but how to delight in God's Word together.

Parenting isn't easy. But when I hear my children talk about God, or when I see them applying Scripture in their own little ways, I'm reminded that He's guiding me, even when I feel unsure. My role is to keep planting seeds of truth. God's role is to make them grow.

He Sees Me, Too

Reflect on your parenting journey today:

- How are you intentionally teaching your children about God and His Word?
- What creative ways could you bring Scripture into your daily routines?
- How might you make faith a joyful, engaging part of your children's lives this week?

Write down your reflections, ideas, or even a small plan for how you'll share God's Word with your children in a new way.

____

____

____

____

____

____

____

____

____

____

____

____

____

____

____

____

____

____

____

____

____

____

____

He Hears Me, Too

Lord, guide me as I raise my children in Your ways. Give me wisdom, patience, and grace in every decision. Help me create a home where Your Word is treasured, taught, and lived out daily. Let my children grow up knowing You personally and loving You deeply. Thank You for trusting me with this calling. In Jesus' Name, Amen.

13

Mercy in the Mess

He Knows Me, Too

It is of the Lord's mercies that we are not consumed, because his compassions fail not. They are new every morning: great is thy faithfulness *(Lamentations 3:22–23, KJV).*

He Feels Me, Too

God's mercies have carried me more times than I can count. Parenting six children, including my twins with autism, I've had moments where I've missed the mark. I've had to fall on my knees, repent, and ask God to realign my heart. Parenting isn't just about authority in the natural—it's also about spiritual authority, raising our children in a way that glorifies God, not our flesh.

I remember when my twins were little, barely toddlers, and they would run from me laughing as if it were a game. My heart would pound, fear gripping me as I chased them, especially in public places or near busy streets. What felt like play to them could have turned tragic in an instant.

One day, I decided to teach them about mercy. I explained that God gives us another chance—not because He has to, but because He loves us and wants us to change. Little by little, I started rewarding their obedience, replacing dangerous choices with positive reinforcement. A favorite toy. A word of encouragement. A celebration of their progress.

But truthfully, it wasn't just about them. God used those moments to check me too. There were times I lost my patience, times I reacted harshly, and later I had to go back, humble myself, and apologize to my children. Mercy wasn't just for them — it was for me. It reminded me that being a better mom sometimes meant laying down pride and picking up grace.

It felt endless at times. If one twin acted out, the other quickly followed. I would wonder, *"Lord, when will this end?"* But in those chaotic, exhausting moments, He whispered, *"My mercies are new every morning. If I can extend mercy to you daily, you can extend it to them."*

And He was right. Day by day, the behavior shifted. Day by day, His faithfulness showed up in our home.

He Sees Me, Too

Take time today to reflect and write:

- Where have you seen God's mercy show up in your parenting?

- Have there been times you needed to go back and apologize to your child, showing them grace?

- How is God's faithfulness sustaining you right now?

Be honest with yourself. Mercy is not weakness; it's a reflection of God's heart through you.

____

____

____

____

____

____

____

____

____

____

____

____

____

____

____

____

____

____

____

____

____

____

____

He Hears Me, Too

Lord, thank You for Your unending faithfulness and mercies that are new every morning. Teach me to parent with the same compassion You show me daily. Help me extend grace even when I feel stretched thin, and remind me to choose mercy over frustration. Guide me with supernatural wisdom in every decision I make for my children. In Jesus' Name, Amen.

14

Grace for My Weak Places

He Knows Me, Too

And he said unto me, My grace is sufficient for thee: for my strength is made perfect in weakness. Most gladly therefore will I rather glory in my infirmities, that the power of Christ may rest upon me *(2 Corinthians 12:9, KJV).*

He Feels Me, Too

There is no room in this season of my life to entertain the enemy's mind games. The moment a negative thought creeps in—whether it's a memory of something a doctor said about my twins, or the whisper of comparison trying to take root—I cast it down and speak God's Word back to Him. He never lies. He never fails. And His grace has always proven to be enough for me.

I remember when doctors told me my boys might struggle to comprehend, that they might not walk or develop like other children. I nodded politely in those appointments, but in my spirit, I said, *"I don't receive that."* Today, those same boys are running, laughing, playing sports, and showing me daily that God has the final say. Their comprehension? Better than anyone expected. Their energy? Overflowing.

It hasn't been easy. There were nights when I felt utterly ill-equipped, wondering if I had what it took to parent them well. But in those moments, God's presence wrapped around me like a blanket. He reminded me that His grace fills the gaps where my strength runs out. He doesn't want me to crumble—He wants me to grow.

I've learned to ask not *"Why me?"* but *"What's the lesson?"* What is God teaching me through this? How is He shaping me to be a better mother—and equipping me to encourage another mom who feels like giving up?

One of the biggest lessons has been grace—not just God's grace for me, but extending grace to my boys. My daughters always seemed ahead, meeting milestones early and excelling with ease. At first, I found myself comparing. But God showed me: *"They are different children with different callings. Don't measure them by the same standards. Celebrate their progress, not their pace."*

Now, I rejoice in the small victories. Every word spoken, every skill gained, every attempt made is a reason to give thanks. As long as they're trying, as long as they're growing, that's what matters. Grace is not lowering the bar—it's trusting that God is writing their story at the right pace.

He Sees Me, Too

Take a moment to sit with God and reflect:

- Where are you feeling weak or inadequate in your parenting?
- How can you invite God's grace to fill those spaces today?
- Are you setting unfair standards on your child — or on yourself? How can you replace comparison with grace?
- Do you have a daily time to abide in God's presence? If not, what small step could you take to begin?

Write honestly. Let this be a place of release, not pressure.

____

____

____

____

He Hears Me, Too

Lord, thank You for Your grace that never runs dry. When I feel weak, remind me that Your strength is made perfect in those very places. Teach me to rest in Your power instead of my own striving. Help me extend grace to my children, to myself, and to others You've called me to encourage. Thank You that Your grace is sufficient for today and every day. In Jesus' Name, Amen.

15

Courage for the Hard Days

He Knows Me, Too

Have not I commanded thee? Be strong and of a good courage; be not afraid, neither be thou dismayed: for the Lord thy God is with thee whithersoever thou goest *(Joshua 1:9, KJV).*

He Feels Me, Too

Parenting a child with special needs is not for the faint of heart. Some days, the journey feels like a battlefield with twists, turns, and unexpected challenges. But I've learned that we are graced for this task. God didn't call us to this assignment without equipping us for the fight. Each morning, I remind myself to put on my warrior gear, to walk with courage, and to remember that God is with me wherever I go.

There were times I had to abandon a shopping cart full of groceries and leave the store because one of my twins "just wasn't having it that day." Crowds overwhelm them. The noise, the lights, the press of bodies moving all around—it can be too much. At first, I felt defeated, like I couldn't take them anywhere. But slowly, I learned to adjust.

Now, I plan around their needs. We shop very early in the morning, when the store aisles are quiet and the air feels calm, or later in the evening, when the crowds have gone and the fluorescent lights hum softly in near-empty aisles. Those times bring peace, and the trip goes smoothly.

It took courage to stop saying, *"I won't go anymore,"* and instead say, *"I'll find another way."* That's what courage looks like for parents like me—not the absence of fear, but the determination to keep showing up, even if it takes extra planning and extra grace.

This journey requires courage because it's not just about grocery trips. It's about standing tall in the face of meltdowns, adjusting schedules for therapy appointments, advocating in schools, and refusing to let discouragement win. God calls it a "light affliction," not because it feels light in the moment, but because compared to the glory He's producing in us, it cannot compare.

So I hold onto Joshua 1:9. I breathe it in like oxygen: *"Be strong and of a good courage…for the Lord thy God is with thee whithersoever thou goest."* And with that promise, I keep pressing forward.

He Sees Me, Too

Take a few minutes to pause and write:

- Where in your journey do you most need courage right now?
- How can you draw strength from God's constant presence instead of your own willpower?
- What is your heart saying when you spend time in His presence?
- Looking ahead, what do you want your journey to look like in the future with Him leading the way?

Let your answers remind you that courage doesn't mean doing it alone — it means walking boldly with God right beside you.

____

____

____

____

He Hears Me, Too

Father, thank You for walking with me through this journey. When I feel weary or overwhelmed, remind me that I can draw courage from You. Thank You for giving me laser-focused strength to complete the assignment You've called me to. Help me not to fear, not to quit, and not to lose sight of Your presence. I trust You to carry me every step of the way. In Jesus' Name, Amen.

16

Standing Still While God Fights for Me

He Knows Me, Too

And Moses said unto the people, Fear ye not, stand still, and see the salvation of the Lord, which he will shew to you to day: for the Egyptians whom ye have seen to day, ye shall see them again no more for ever. The Lord shall fight for you, and ye shall hold your peace *(Exodus 14:13–14, KJV).*

He Feels Me, Too

As a mother of twins on the spectrum, I take comfort in knowing that God is fighting battles I can't even see. He is the Potter, and He knows exactly what He placed inside me to equip me for this calling. I may not always feel capable, but He reminds me daily that I am.

People often ask, *"How do you do it with twins?"* My answer is always the same: *"By God's grace, one day at a time—sometimes one moment at a time."* Because truthfully, this life is not for the faint of heart. It takes strength that can only come from Him.

I've learned not to expect people to always understand. Many can't imagine what it's like to walk in my shoes. Some are too caught up in their own worlds to notice when you need help. Others judge without compassion. I remember one of my neighbors once asked, "They aren't potty trained yet?" When I explained they were on the spectrum, her entire demeanor shifted. That moment reminded me how quick people are to judge without knowing the full story.

And that's the thing, the world may not understand, but God does. People may judge the meltdowns, the late milestones, the moments that don't look like everyone else's, but God sees deeper. He's not standing in judgment; He's standing in battle on our behalf.

So I rest in His Word: *"Stand still, and see the salvation of the Lord."* My job is not to fight every critic or carry every weight. My job is to trust Him, to hold my peace, and to believe that He will win battles I could never fight on my own.

Every time I've surrendered, I've watched Him move—not always instantly, but always faithfully. He has promised healing and restoration for my boys, and I know He will do it. My part is to stand still in faith.

He Sees Me, Too

Take a few moments to reflect and write:

- What battles are you facing right now as a parent of a special needs child?
- Where are you trying to fight in your own strength instead of letting God go to bat for you?
- What promises from God are you holding onto in this season for your child(ren)?

Be honest. Lay the burdens down on paper as an act of surrender.

____

____

____

____

____

____

____

____

____

____

____
____
____
____
____
____
____
____
____
____

He Hears Me, Too

Lord, thank You for being my defender and the One who fights for me. Thank You for the measure of faith You've poured into me to stand even when I feel weary. I trust You to make all things new and beautiful in Your timing. I believe in the miracles You have promised for my children and me, and I thank You now for total restoration. In Jesus' Name, Amen.

17

When Glory Walked into the Room

He Knows Me, Too

And he said, I beseech thee, shew me thy glory *(Exodus 33:18, KJV).*

He Feels Me, Too

When I think of God's glory, I think of His power manifested right here on earth — undeniable, breathtaking, unstoppable. And I have seen it with my own eyes through my children, especially my twins.

I'll never forget the day Kayden started speaking in full sentences. His voice filled the room, words flowing freely where once there had only been silence. Soon after, I watched him run across the yard, soccer ball at his feet, his laughter carried on the breeze. I cried until I couldn't cry anymore. I thought back to the hospital the day they were born—to the reports that said they would never hear, never speak. And yet, here he was. Living, breathing proof of God's glory.

The day they were born, the doctors kept insisting something was wrong. They ran hearing screenings over and over, shaking their heads, whispering words like *"deaf"* and *"mute."* They wanted to keep them in observation, to run more tests. I had just had my fifth C-section, barely three hours out of surgery, but something in my spirit rose up. I started packing our things. I knew what God had told me: *"They will hear. They will talk."*

Throughout my pregnancy, I had laid hands on my belly and placed headphones with gospel music over them. I prayed, declaring life over their ears, their voices, their futures. And I refused to accept any report that didn't align with God's promise.

A week later, we went back. The doctor was shocked. "They're not deaf," he said in disbelief. The audiologist confirmed it—their hearing was perfect.

That was God's glory. Not just in the healing, but in the faith that carried me through when everything around me said otherwise.

And it hasn't stopped. Every milestone, every unexpected breakthrough, every answered prayer has been another glimpse of His glory revealed.

He Sees Me, Too

Take a quiet moment to reflect and write:

- Where have you seen glimpses of God's glory in your parenting journey?

- What promises has He given you about your children that you are still holding onto?

- How are you putting a demand on His Word while also doing your part in faith?

Let this be your reminder: His glory is not a one-time event. It is unfolding, daily, in ways you may not even see yet.

____

____

____

____

____

____

____

____

____

____

____

____

____

____

____

____

____

____

____

____

He Hears Me, Too

Lord, I thank You for Your glory being manifested in my life and in the lives of my children. Thank You for covering us, for silencing every false report, and for reminding me that You alone have the final say. Help me to walk in expectation of Your power, believing that the best is yet to come. May Your glory shine through our lives as a testimony to others. In Jesus' Name, Amen.

18

When Mercy Meets My Mess

He Knows Me, Too

Be merciful, just as your Father is merciful *(Luke 6:36, NIV)*.

He Feels Me, Too

When I think of God's mercy, I see the Cross. I see Jesus taking on all my sins, all my shortcomings, and covering me with a love I could never earn. I see Him as a faithful Father, always ready to forgive, always ready to draw me back into His arms.

That same mercy is what sustains me as a parent—especially as a mother of twins on the spectrum.

There is no handbook for raising children, and even less guidance for raising special needs children. Some days, I don't get it right. I've had moments where I yelled, moments of discouragement so deep I felt like I was failing, moments where I collapsed under the weight of it all. But every time, God met me there with mercy.

When my twins turned two, I braced myself for the "terrible twos." But what I didn't know then was that for many special needs parents, that stage doesn't just pass. It lingers. And sometimes, it feels like it never ends.

With my girls, tantrums lasted maybe ten minutes—whining, kicking, a few tears, then it was over. But with the boys, it was a different reality. Meltdowns came full force: screaming so high-pitched it pierced the air, bodies flinging into walls and doors until holes were left behind, throwing themselves to the ground in public with no regard for stares, crying for an hour straight with no sign of stopping. I've walked out of rooms trembling, praying under my breath, "Lord, have mercy."

And He did. Every single time.

His mercy didn't always change the situation instantly, but it changed me. It gave me the strength to keep showing up, to keep loving, to keep trying again. Mercy reminded me that I wasn't parenting alone. Mercy reminded me that even in my weakest moments, God's arms were strong enough to hold us all.

He Sees Me, Too

Take a moment to reflect and write:

- Where in your parenting journey have you desperately needed God's mercy?
- Did you surrender it all to Him: the frustration, the fear, the exhaustion?
- What changes did you notice after God's mercy met you in those moments?

Write openly, even about the hard parts. Mercy is found in honesty, not perfection.

____

____

____

____

____

____

____

____

____

____

____

____

____

____

____

____

____

____

____

____

He Hears Me, Too

Lord, thank You for Your mercy that meets me in my weakest moments. Thank You for never turning me away when I fall short. Give me the grace to parent with patience and love, even on the hardest days. Remind me that I can always come back to You for the strength and refilling I need. You are my Mercy and my Strength. In Jesus' Name, Amen.

19

Beauty Rising from the Ashes

He Knows Me, Too

and provide for those who grieve in Zion—to bestow on them a crown of beauty instead of ashes, the oil of joy instead of mourning, and a garment of praise instead of a spirit of despair. They will be called oaks of righteousness, a planting of the Lord for the display of his splendor *(Isaiah 61:3, NIV)*.

He Feels Me, Too

There was a season when the ashes in my life felt overwhelming. My twins were small, barely walking, and silence filled our home where baby babbles should have been. Day after day, I waited to hear their voices—a giggle, a word, a sound—but nothing came. I compared them to my older children, remembering the milestones they hit, and my heart sank lower each time.

I would cry silently, feeling devastated and defeated. Torment became my constant companion. I hovered over them, checking their breathing with mirrors on their noses, examining their bodies for cuts or bruises, even their hair and teeth—desperate to make sure nothing was wrong. When they started school, I was terrified because they couldn't tell me if someone touched them or hurt them. Fear consumed me until God broke through with a whisper: *"Stop worrying. Get them tested. Begin early intervention. And watch Me work a miracle."*

I obeyed, even through my tears. And just three months later, the ashes began to turn into beauty. My boys started walking, running, and one of them began speaking single words. I cried tears of joy this time, overwhelmed by the evidence of God's promise.

Now, I see their smiles when they run into school, eager to see their therapists and friends. The torment that once clouded my mind has lifted. God freed me, not just from fear but from despair. He showed me that even in the ashes of what I thought I'd lost, His beauty was rising.

Every day, their progress reminds me: God restores. He redeems. He turns mourning into dancing. And He is giving me beauty for ashes.

He Sees Me, Too

Take time today to reflect and write:

- Are you walking through ashes right now, or do you see beauty beginning to rise?
- What has God redeemed in your life this past year—in parenting, purpose, finances, or your own heart?
- Where have you seen Him replace torment with peace, or despair with joy?

Write it down as a testimony, so you can look back and remember His faithfulness.

____

____

____

____

____

____

____

____

____

____

____

____

____

____

____

____

____

____

____

____

He Hears Me, Too

Lord, thank You for never throwing us away, even in our weakness and doubt. Thank You for loving me with a love that never fails. I praise You for redeeming my time, restoring what I thought was lost, and turning my ashes into beauty. You are the Ultimate Restorer and Rewarder, and I trust You to continue the good work You have begun. In Jesus' Name, Amen.

20

The Double Portion of Grace

He Knows Me, Too

Instead of your shame you will receive a double portion, and instead of disgrace you will rejoice in your inheritance. And so you will inherit a double portion in your land, and everlasting joy will be yours *(Isaiah 61:7, NIV).*

He Feels Me, Too

Parenting children with special needs often feels like needing a double of everything: double time, double patience, double hands, and above all, double grace. And the truth is—God provides it.

I'll never forget one evening at a crowded restaurant. My family had just settled in, menus spread across the table, when my twins suddenly erupted. Screaming at the tops of their lungs. Kicking. Throwing food across the floor. The sound cut through the chatter of the room until every head turned toward us. Faces filled with disgust. Some shook their heads. No one offered help. No one asked if we were okay. They just stared.

Heat rose in my cheeks, shame pressing down like a heavy blanket. My other children looked embarrassed, their eyes pleading with me to make it stop. I hurried to calm the boys, but nothing worked. Finally, we left in the middle of dinner, my heart breaking as I pushed them out the door.

And then, as we stepped outside, they were suddenly fine. Quiet. Smiling. As if nothing had happened. That's when I heard God's voice loud and clear: *"Don't you ever leave a place again because of the people's faces."*

That moment changed me.

Now, when they cry or act out in public, I don't let shame drive me away. I don't let fear of stares control our family. We stay. We finish our meal. We keep living. My older children talk and laugh, and I remain unbothered. Because the truth is, I'm not living for the approval of strangers—I'm living under the covering of a God who promised me a double portion.

The double portion was freedom: freedom from fear, from shame, from torment, from constantly wondering what others think. And in its place, He gave us grace. Grace to enjoy family time. Grace to rest in His presence. Grace to stand strong in the calling of parenting these precious boys.

He Sees Me, Too

Pause today and reflect:

- Where in your parenting journey have you felt shame—and how has God replaced it with grace?
- Can you recall a moment where God gave you "double"—double strength, double patience, or double joy?
- What would it look like for you to stop worrying about "people's faces" and start living in God's freedom?

Write it out. Put Him in remembrance of His goodness, and remind yourself of the history you and God already share.

____

____

____

____

____

____

____

____

____

____

____

____

____

____

____

____

____

____

____

____

He Hears Me, Too

Lord, thank You for being my strength and my freedom. Thank You for the double portion of grace You give me daily to parent with courage. Help me release shame and walk boldly in the joy You have promised. Let my family be a testimony of Your goodness, and remind me that in You, we never leave empty. In Jesus' Name, Amen.

21

When the Weight Feels Too Much

He Knows Me, Too

The Lord is close to the brokenhearted and saves those who are crushed in spirit *(Psalm 34:18, NIV).*

He Feels Me, Too

There are days when the weight of it all nearly knocks me down. As a single mother of six—with a full-time job and twins on the spectrum—exhaustion sometimes feels like a constant shadow. On those days, the responsibilities stack so high I can barely see past them. The meltdowns, the sleepless nights, the isolation of not being able to just "go out" like other families—it presses in until my spirit feels crushed.

I call these my human moments.

In those moments, I feel heavy. So heavy that I wonder if I'll ever find my way back to joy. But I've learned not to stay there long. Because even when the heaviness wraps itself around me, I know the truth: God is close. He is right there, whispering comfort when I feel alone, holding me together when I want to fall apart.

There are times I sit quietly and remind Him of His promises over my children—of their healing, their restoration, their freedom. And as I speak His Word back to Him, something shifts inside me. The heaviness begins to lift. The tears dry. My heart steadies.

I don't always see the answers right away, but I've learned to find joy in the waiting. Not because the journey is easy, but because I know I'm not carrying it alone.

He Sees Me, Too

Take a moment today to reflect and write:

- What part of your parenting journey feels heaviest right now?

- How has God's presence met you in your "human moments"?

- In what ways has your heaviness shaped you into a

stronger, more compassionate parent?

- Where do you feel God calling you to trust Him more deeply?

Be real with yourself. Honesty is the first step toward healing.

He Hears Me, Too

Lord, I bring the weight of my heart to You. When I feel crushed, remind me that You are near. Thank You for never putting more on me than I can bear, and for trusting me with this assignment. Give me the grace to keep moving forward in love and faith as I parent my children. I choose not to complain, but to lean on You. Thank You for being my strength when I feel heavy. In Jesus' Name, Amen.

22

Chosen for This Calling

He Knows Me, Too

And we know that in all things God works for the good of those who love him, who have been called according to his purpose *(Romans 8:28, NIV).*

He Feels Me, Too

I am so grateful that God chose me. He chose me to parent the children I have, and He entrusted me with the assignments that no one else can fulfill. Every day, even when the weight feels heavy, I remind myself: I am called. I am chosen.

When I first learned my twins had autism, I wasn't completely surprised. Working in the mental health field, I had seen the signs and done my research. I knew early intervention was crucial, so I reached out for resources and support right away. But in my heart, I also sensed something deeper.

I remember saying to God, *"You must want me to expand in this area. This isn't just about me. This isn't just about them. There's a bigger purpose here."* And He answered, *"Yes. It is."*

What some would call a light affliction, I came to understand as a divine assignment. My journey wasn't meant to break me — it was meant to build me, to prepare me to help others find hope, healing, and light. This devotional isn't just for me. It's for you, too. For your healing. For your deliverance.

Even when we don't see how it all fits together, God is working behind the scenes. Nothing is wasted. Not the tears. Not the late nights. Not the prayers whispered through exhaustion. He weaves it all for our good and for His glory.

So I ask myself daily: Am I looking at the glass half empty or half full? Am I choosing life? Am I living as one who is called and chosen? The answer has to be yes—because if God chose me, then He has already equipped me.

He Sees Me, Too

Take time today to reflect and write:

- Do you truly believe that you are called and chosen for this assignment of parenting your child(ren)?
- Are you viewing your situation through the lens of God's purpose, or through the lens of defeat?
- How can you shift your perspective today to see the bigger picture of what God is doing?

Write honestly. This is your reminder: being chosen means your life and your parenting have purpose far beyond what you can see right now.

____

____

____

____

____

____

____

____

____

____

____

____

____

____

____

____

____

____

____

____

He Hears Me, Too

Lord, thank You for calling and choosing me for this assignment. Even when I feel unprepared or overwhelmed, remind me that You equipped me before I ever knew the task. Help me to walk in confidence, grace, and faith, knowing that all things are working for my good and for Your glory. In Jesus' Name, Amen.

23

Trusting When the Road Is Unclear

He Knows Me, Too

Trust in the Lord with all your heart and lean not on your own understanding; in all your ways submit to him, and he will make your paths straight *(Proverbs 3:5–6, NIV).*

He Feels Me, Too

Every day, I make the choice not to crumble. Not to stay in bed. Not to let the heaviness win. Some mornings, I wake up exhausted, but the moment I sit with God, I feel the strength to rise and face the day. That quiet time — even if it's just a few minutes—anchors me. It reminds me that I'm not walking this road alone.

People ask me often, *"How do you do it? How do you manage as a single working mom of six, with twins on the spectrum?"* My answer is always the same: *"It's Jesus. It's the Holy Spirit leading me every step of the way."* Because if I relied on my own strength, I'd be curled up somewhere in tears. But God gives me the courage to keep living, to keep pressing forward, to keep believing that my twins are healed—even as I wait for the full manifestation of His promise.

One memory stays with me. A therapist once told me that only one of my twins would benefit from an AAC tablet, and the other would have to wait. Something in my spirit rose up: *"No. They will both have the same opportunity. They are both capable. They will both thrive."*

At first, insurance said they'd only cover one. But God told me to trust Him and push forward. So I did. And not long after, the call came — both were approved. If I had leaned on the therapist's word instead of God's, one of my sons would have been left behind. But trusting Him made the path straight.

There are still moments when I wonder, *"Why me? Why my children?"* But I've learned not to camp there. That road leads to torment. Instead, I remind myself: God knows the path. He knows the "why" even when I don't. My job is to trust

Him, even when it doesn't make sense. Because in His hands, every rough road leads to beauty, every trial to testimony.

He Sees Me, Too

Take time today to reflect and write:

- What areas of your parenting journey feel unclear right now?
- Where is God asking you to trust Him more deeply instead of leaning on your own understanding?
- Can you look back and see a moment where trusting God changed the outcome? Write it down as a reminder that He is faithful.

Let this reflection be an act of surrender, laying down the weight of the unknown in exchange for His peace.

____

____

____

____

____

____

____

____

____

____

____

____

____

____

____

____

____

____

____

____

He Hears Me, Too

Lord, I give total surrender to You—my life, my children, and every detail of our journey. When the road feels rough and unclear, remind me that You are guiding each step. Help me lean on Your strength instead of my own understanding. Thank You for having a perfect plan for me and my children, and for making our paths straight. In Jesus' Name, Amen.

24

Laying It All Down

He Knows Me, Too

Cast your cares on the Lord and he will sustain you; he will never let the righteous be shaken *(Psalm 55:22, NIV).*

He Feels Me, Too

As a special needs mom, my life is a daily practice of handing my thoughts and actions back to God. I want Him to be pleased first, even above my own expectations, and I long to be the best parent I can for my children.

But if I'm honest, some of my hardest moments come in public. Grocery stores, parks, restaurants—they can feel like battlefields. The enemy whispers lies: *"Just stay home. Don't even try. They're going to act up. People will stare. You'll be embarrassed again."*

For a while, I let those thoughts win. I stayed home, shrinking my world smaller and smaller. But then God spoke to me: *"Don't let fear write your story."*

Now, I intentionally make it a point to take my twins out every single day—even if it's just a quick walk in the park or a run to the store. I choose to expose them to the world instead of hiding them from it. Yes, there are meltdowns. Yes, there are stares. But I've stopped letting other people's opinions weigh more than God's promises.

Little by little, I've seen progress. The boys are adjusting more easily to external stimuli, and I'm growing stronger in my resolve. I no longer care about the stares—my focus is on raising my children in faith, with patience, and under the covering of God's grace. He is my source. He sustains me. He carries the weight I was never meant to bear alone.

Every day, I remind myself: I am not shaken, because God is holding me steady.

He Sees Me, Too

Take a moment today to release what's heavy on your heart:

- What fears or anxieties have been pressing on you as a parent?
- Are there lies the enemy has been whispering that

you need to cast down today?

- How can you intentionally give those burdens to God and step forward in faith instead of retreating in fear?

Write them down. Name them. Then lay them at the feet of Jesus and refuse to pick them back up.

He Hears Me, Too

Lord, I thank You for being my safe place and my strength. Thank You for protecting me and my children and for surrounding us with Your love and favor. Help me to release every anxious thought and overwhelming burden into Your hands. Sustain me daily, and remind me that I was never meant to carry this alone. In Jesus' Name, Amen.

25

Grace Upon Grace

He Knows Me, Too

But he said to me, 'My grace is sufficient for you, for my power is made perfect in weakness.' Therefore I will boast all the more gladly about my weaknesses, so that Christ's power may rest on me. That is why, for Christ's sake, I delight in weaknesses, in insults, in hardships, in persecutions, in difficulties. For when I am weak, then I am strong *(2 Corinthians 12:9–10, NIV).*

He Feels Me, Too

Parenting my twins has shown me more clearly than anything else just how much I need God's grace. There were days I would stand in my backyard, tears stinging my eyes, yelling into the open air because I felt so frustrated. I didn't understand their wiring, their processing, or why the meltdowns felt endless. I didn't know how to carry the weight.

One of those days, I remember crying out, *"Lord, I can't do this anymore!"* And in the stillness that followed, I felt Him whisper, *"These things will pass."*

And they did.

Now, instead of screaming into the backyard, I turn to my Bible. I open its pages and find God waiting there with fresh grace. I whisper prayers like, *"God, please give me more grace for today—more grace for parenting, more grace for patience, more grace for whatever this journey brings."* And He has never failed me. Not once.

Even on the hardest days, His grace has covered me like a blanket, quieting the frustration and giving me strength I didn't know I had. My neighbors may be relieved that they no longer hear me screaming outside, but I'm more relieved that I've found a better way—resting in the arms of a God who always meets me where I am.

Because the truth is this: my weakness doesn't disqualify me. It's the very place where God's power shows up strongest.

He Sees Me, Too

Take time today to reflect and write:

- Where do you feel weakest in your parenting right now?
- How has God's grace shown up in those weak places?
- What specific prayer for "more grace" can you bring to Him today?

Let your journaling be an honest place of surrender—not polished, just real.

____

____

____

____

____

____

____

____

____

____

____

____

____

____

____

____

____

____

____

____

He Hears Me, Too

Lord, thank You for Your grace upon grace as I parent my children. Thank You for showing me the good, even when things don't turn out the way I planned. Strengthen my mind and spirit, and let me be the role model my children need. Cover me daily with Your power, and remind me that when I am weak, I am strong in You. In Jesus' Name, Amen.

26

Courage That Conquers Fear

He Knows Me, Too

Be strong and courageous. Do not be afraid or terrified because of them, for the Lord your God goes with you; he will never leave you nor forsake you *(Deuteronomy 31:6, NIV).*

He Feels Me, Too

As a special needs mom, fear has often tried to creep in and tell me what I can and cannot do. The enemy whispers lies: *"You won't be able to handle it. They'll act up. You'll be embarrassed. You don't have enough help."* But I've learned this—when God is with me, fear has no power.

I remember the first time I planned to take my kids out of town for a family trip. Everything in me wanted to back down. The enemy kept taunting me: *"Cancel it. Stay home. You know how this will go."* But I pushed back in faith, booked the trip, and told Satan to shut up. We were going—and nothing was going to stop us.

We flew to Chicago in the summer for the Taste of Chicago festival, a massive event where people from all over the world gather. I started preparing with wisdom: cooling blankets for the heat, whistles in case of emergencies, helmets for protection. I problem-solved, but I also prayed—asking God to cover every step.

On the flight, I had let the airline know I was traveling with multiple children, including my 3-year-old twins. By God's favor, we ended up in first class, quiet and calm. The flight attendants brought us snacks, and because it was a nighttime flight, the twins slept the entire time. Not a single issue.

When we first arrived, the boys had a meltdown for about an hour. My flesh wanted to panic, but instead, I laid hands, rebuked the enemy, and prayed. Within moments, peace fell, and they were fine for the rest of the week. We enjoyed our trip, made memories, and proved once again that God keeps His Word.

That trip taught me a valuable lesson: I will never let the devil punk me out of what God has promised. Fear doesn't get the final say. God does.

Now, I walk in courage as a parent, knowing that I have dominion and authority—not because of who I am, but because of whose I am. I am a King's kid. My children are His, and our steps are ordered.

He Sees Me, Too

Reflect today and write:

- Where has fear tried to bully you in your parenting?
- What steps can you take to push back against fear with faith and preparation?
- What are you believing God for this year in your children's lives? Write it down. Stand on it. Pray over it daily.

Let your words be your stand of faith.

____

____

____

____

____

____

____

____

____

____

____

____

____

____

____

____

____

____

____

____

He Hears Me, Too

Lord, I thank You for boldness and courage as I walk this journey of parenting. Thank You for making my paths straight and for always keeping Your promises. Help me to live free from fear, knowing that You go before me in every step I take. I trust You with my children's future and with my own. Everything will be made new in Your perfect timing. In Jesus' Name, Amen.

27

The Work Isn't Finished Yet

He Knows Me, Too

Being confident of this, that he who began a good work in you will carry it on to completion until the day of Christ Jesus *(Philippians 1:6, NIV).*

He Feels Me, Too

Parenting children on the spectrum has taught me the beauty of celebrating small victories—because in God's eyes, they aren't small at all. Every step forward, every breakthrough, is evidence of His good work continuing in us.

I'll never forget the day Kayden looked at me and said, *"I love you, Mommy."*

We had just left church, the sun warm on our backs as we walked to the parking lot. His voice came suddenly, unexpected, like a melody I had been waiting years to hear. At first, I thought I imagined it. But then he said it again. And again.

I froze. Tears blurred my vision as I tried to take in the moment. We stood there in that nearly empty parking lot for ten minutes, my other children wrapping their arms around me as I cried. Kayden kept repeating those three words, and each time, it felt like a piece of heaven had broken into my ordinary day.

It was a reminder: God's work is still unfolding. Slowly but surely. Step by step. Miracle by miracle.

That day, I couldn't help but worship right there in my car after the service. God was showing me what He promised long ago—that He had not forgotten me or my children. And the progress I see now is only the beginning.

When I look back to where we were last year, I can't help but thank God. Because the milestones, the growth, the victories — they are proof that the One who began a good work in us is faithful to complete it.

He Sees Me, Too

Take time today to reflect and write:

- Where were you this time last year in your parenting journey?
- What milestones or victories—big or small—can you celebrate since then?
- How does remembering your progress help you press forward with faith into what's next?

Don't skip over the little things. Write them down as evidence that God is working, even now.

____

____

____

____

____

____

____

____

____

____

____

____

He Hears Me, Too

Lord, I am amazed at how far You have brought me. Thank You for every milestone, every answered prayer, every step forward. I know I could not have done this without You. I am forever grateful for the expansion in our lives and the progress we've made so far. I wait in expectation for what You will do next year and beyond. In Jesus' Name, Amen.

28

Help Is on the Way

He Knows Me, Too

I lift up my eyes to the mountains—where does my help come from? My help comes from the Lord, the Maker of heaven and earth *(Psalm 121:1–2, NIV).*

He Feels Me, Too

Parenting my twins has taught me this truth again and again: my help comes from the Lord. Not from people, not from my own strength, but from the One who made heaven and earth.

I've seen His help in so many ways. When the tantrums began to lessen. When nights once filled with crying turned into peaceful sleep. When the boys started running, laughing, and playing with other kids instead of sitting on the sidelines. When their words began to flow clearly—and the day in the church parking lot when Kayden looked at me and said, *"I love you, Mommy."*

That day, the sermon had been about not giving up in trials. As we walked to the car, his words pierced my heart like a beam of light through the clouds. I knew it wasn't just Kayden speaking—it was God reminding me, *"I see you. I'm with you. Don't give up."*

But there are other moments too— harder ones. Like when Kayden began asking about his father. His little eyes searched mine as he asked questions I wasn't sure how to answer. Finally, I told him the truth: *"Your dad is in heaven now."* I reminded him that Jesus is his Father too, that he can always talk to Him, that the Holy Spirit is his constant guide.

Later that night, I prayed. *"Lord, please send strong, godly men to mentor my boys. Give them examples to look up to, men who will love them and lead them well."*

That's what God's help looks like—not just solving problems, but sending exactly what we need in every season.

Parenting isn't about being a superhero. It's about knowing when to lift your eyes and ask for help—and trusting that God will send it, whether through His Spirit, His Word, or His people.

He Sees Me, Too

Take time today to reflect and write:

- Where do you need God's help most in this season of parenting?
- Have you been trying to carry too much on your own instead of lifting it to Him?
- Make a list of tasks or burdens you can delegate or release—and then pray over them, asking God for His divine help and connections.

Remember: you weren't meant to carry this load alone.

____

____

____

____

____

____

____

____

____

____

____

____

____

____

____

____

____

____

____

____

He Hears Me, Too

Lord, thank You for being my ever-present help. Thank You for providing divine strength, supernatural connections, and the peace I need to parent well. Surround my children with Your love, and send the right people to pour into their lives as they grow. Help me remember that I don't have to do this alone—because You are always with us. In Jesus' Name, Amen.

29

Secured by His Care

He Knows Me, Too

Cast all your anxiety on him because he cares for you *(1 Peter 5:7, NIV).*

He Feels Me, Too

As a special needs mom, the "what ifs" used to torment me. *What will happen to my children when I'm gone? Who will take care of them? Where will they live? Will they be safe?*

For a while, those thoughts weighed me down until I realized worry wouldn't solve anything. Instead, I needed to take action with wisdom while laying every anxious thought before God.

The Holy Spirit led me to start preparing—not in fear, but in faith. I opened savings accounts for each of my children, including Uniform Transfers to Minors Act (UTMA) accounts and Roth Individual Retirement Account (Roth IRAs). Later, God placed it on my heart to set up a special needs trust, ensuring that my boys would be cared for without fear of exploitation. I learned about Achieving a Better Life Experience (ABLE) accounts, group home care, and other resources designed to protect them.

One step at a time, I began building a legacy plan—knowing this wasn't just about finances, but about stewardship and obedience. And with each step, the burden of worry lifted a little more.

God reminded me: *"You don't carry this alone. I care for you, and I care for them."*

Now, I can rest knowing their future is not only in His hands spiritually, but also secured practically.

He Sees Me, Too

Take time today to reflect and write:

- What fears about your children's future have you been carrying?

- What practical steps can you take this week (like setting up an account, consulting a lawyer, or designating a guardian)?

- How can you invite the Holy Spirit into those plans so that they are covered in prayer as well as preparation?

Let this be a moment of surrender and strategy.

He Hears Me, Too

Lord, I thank You that my children's future is safe in Your hands. Thank You for guiding me in wisdom to make plans that will bless and protect them long after I'm gone. Lift every burden of worry and replace it with peace, knowing that You are their ultimate Father and Protector. In Jesus' Name, Amen.

30

Never Forsaken

He Knows Me, Too

Keep your lives free from the love of money and be content with what you have, because God has said,"Never will I leave you; never will I forsake you *(Hebrews 13:5, NIV).*

He Feels Me, Too

There were seasons when I felt like I was doing this parenting journey all alone. As a single mom of six, I would often ask myself, *"Where can I find time to breathe? To rest? To just be?"*

One day, I asked God for a way to recharge without neglecting my children. The Holy Spirit gave me wisdom. While my twins were in their occupational therapy sessions, I began carving out small windows of time—a quick ice cream stop, a nail appointment, or even just sitting quietly with God in the car.

Those little breaks made a world of difference. I realized that God had never left me; He was simply teaching me how to find rest in the middle of the chaos. Where there is God's will, there is always a way.

Now I no longer see self-care as selfish. I see it as stewardship—filling myself up so I can pour back into my children and others around me. And I hold tightly to the promise that no matter how isolated I may feel, God is right here. He has never left me, and He never will.

He Sees Me, Too

Take a moment to reflect and write:

- When was the last time you felt God's presence in a season of isolation?

- How can you carve out time for rest and renewal, even if it's in small ways?

- Do you need to realign with Him through prayer and repentance so you can hear His voice more clearly?

Write it down and make a plan to lean into His presence this week.

He Hears Me, Too

Lord, thank You for never leaving or forsaking me. Thank You for walking beside me daily and giving me wisdom to parent with strength and grace. Help me carve out moments to rest in Your presence and to recharge so I can pour back into my children. I choose to trust You with my life and theirs, knowing You will never let us go. In Jesus' Name, Amen.

Acknowledgements

First and foremost, I want to extend my deepest gratitude to God, whose unwavering love and guidance have made this journey possible. Your wisdom has been my cornerstone, and I am continually humbled by the grace You have bestowed upon me. Thank You for inspiring me to share Your message and for giving me strength during times of challenge.

To my spiritual parents, your leadership and support have been invaluable. Thank you for nurturing my spirit and providing me with guidance as I endeavor to fulfill God's agenda. Your commitment to spreading His heart to others has shown me the profound impact that love and faith can have in the world. I am grateful for your wisdom and encouragement, which have helped me grow both spiritually and professionally.

To my family, thank you for being my rock and safe haven. Your love, patience, and encouragement have sustained me throughout this journey, reminding me of the importance of unity and support. Each of you has played a vital role in shaping the messages shared in this book, and I am deeply thankful for the countless moments of joy and love that have inspired these pages.

I also want to acknowledge all the special needs families who have shared their stories and experiences with me. Your courage and resilience inspire me daily, reminding me of the beauty that exists in our differences. May this devotional serve as a source of hope and encouragement for you.

About The Author

Nicole Powers, MSN, PMHNP-BC, is first and foremost a devoted daughter of God and a mother of six, including fraternal twin boys diagnosed with autism who inspire much of her advocacy and work. She is a board-certified Psychiatric Mental Health Nurse Practitioner and an autonomous practitioner dedicated to providing compassionate, evidence-based care.

As the founder of Powerful Minds Psychiatry, a thriving telemedicine practice, and the owner of a home care agency, Nicole has built a career rooted in both innovation and service. She also serves as a preceptor, mentoring the next generation of Physician Assistants and Nurse Practitioners with a commitment to excellence in mental health care.

Her authorship of *Autism Is a Superpower* reflects her passion for destigmatizing autism and celebrating the unique strengths of children on the spectrum.

Her second book, *From 0 to 300 Clients in 30 Days*, is a step-by-step guide designed to help healthcare professionals—nurses, nurse practitioners, therapists, and other providers—build visibility, attract clients, and grow their practice with confidence. In addition to her writing, she has delivered impactful talks on autism, equipping families and communities with knowledge, hope, and advocacy tools.

Nicole's journey embodies faith, perseverance, and purpose. Through her professional expertise, personal testimony, and unwavering devotion to God, she continues to inspire and uplift those she serves.

Connect with Nicole Powers

Stay connected and join a growing community of parents, caretakers, and advocates walking this road together.

Website: www.powerfulmindspsychiatry.com

Instagram: @nicolethenp_

Facebook: Nicole Powers

www.ingramcontent.com/pod-product-compliance
Lightning Source LLC
LaVergne TN
LVHW050632100826
845148LV00011B/1836

* 9 7 9 8 9 5 0 0 5 3 0 2 3 *